I0531175

WISDOM
— FOR A *New* —
WORLD

100 MESSAGES TO AWAKEN
YOUR HIGHEST SELF

LEANNE BABCOCK

Wisdom for a New World
100 Messages to Awaken Your Higher Self

Copyright © 2025 Leanne Babcock

All rights reserved. No part of this publication may be reproduced, distributed, or transmitted in any form or by any means, including photocopying, recording, or other electronic or mechanical methods, without the prior written permission of the copyright holder, except in the case of brief quotations embodied in critical reviews and certain other noncommercial uses permitted by copyright law.

ISBN: 979-8-9931662-8-5

Book Design by Transcendent Publishing
Editing by Catherine Cooper and Sara Gavrell
Illustrations by Bĕtka Spring

Printed in the United States of America.

This book is dedicated to
love on the planet.

Table of Contents

Acknowledgments

Wisdom for a New World was a team effort. With my whole heart I thank …

Bětka Spring – graphic artist extraordinaire, who designed each image for every quote.

Catherine Cooper – my writing coach, main editor, and dear friend who always guides me in my writing ways.

George MacPherson – my life partner, who loves me and has limitless patience with me as I get up in the wee hours of the morning to write, and who makes all the dinners when I'm busy at work all day long.

Jen Clarke – who manages all the logistics of my online programs. Thank the heavens for Jen. She holds it all together so I can be totally present in the conversation at hand.

Participants in my courses – these messages come through because of you. This is a deep conversation we engage in together to EXPAND: our hearts, who we are, and our expression in the world.

Sara Gavrell – a client and friend. Who also happens to be a university professor with a darn good eye for detail and editing.

Shanda Trofe – whose guidance for publishing I have trusted for years.

Source – my direct connection with my highest wisdom. Thank you for these messages.

A Word from the Author

Wisdom For a New World is a collection of living teachings from my journeys, my programs, my coaching, and my books.

Use this book as a doorway into deeper wisdom: breathe a question into your heart, open the book to a page, and allow the words to reveal to you what you are ready to hear.

May these messages stir your spirit, expand your vision, and open you to a deeper truth of who you are.

Love,
Leanne

Am I willing to face
my fears and no longer
run from them?

#1
Fear

Maybe it's time to ask yourself, "Am I willing to face my fears, the ones I've carried for lifetimes? Am I willing to no longer run from them? Am I willing to stand and look my fears in the eye…and just let them be without doing anything to change them?"

Holding on to your fears keeps you in the illusion of believing you are alone and separate. This leaves you vulnerable to giving your power away and being manipulated by others.

It takes courage to stop running. When you face your fears, they begin to dissolve…and what opens up is peace.

When you ask for guidance, it is you reaching for information from your Higher Self.

#2
Your Higher Self

Everything is energy, and you are an energy being. You are picking up on energy whether you are aware of it or not. Your intuition is working constantly.

As you become more conscious to your intuition and work with it intentionally, you will sometimes reach for insights and messages that help you.

When you ask for guidance, it is you reaching for information from your Higher Self.

Remember your intuition is simply your navigation system. You have free will to choose.

If your intuition is your navigation system, where could you use it more in your life?

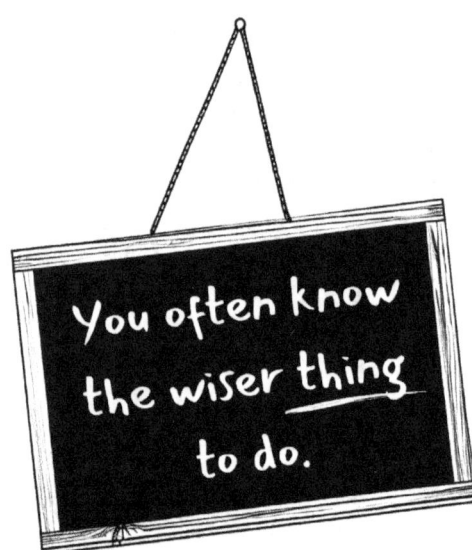

#3
You Know

You often know the wiser thing to do, but sometimes you don't do it. You're not bad. You're not wrong. You're just going to learn that lesson again.

There will come a time, when you will make a different choice. A wiser choice.

Have compassion for yourself. There might be a reason drawing you to the less wise path.

Could there be a hidden gift, or unmet need, or unhealed wound influencing your choice?

You will find your way.

You are not
your thoughts.

#4
You Are Not Your Thoughts

Thoughts are created from the brain's interpretation of sensory input and prior experience.

The brain learns how to think just like the body learns how to walk. As the body and brain learn, these processes become habits.

You are not a habit. You are not your body. You are not your thoughts.

You are divine consciousness. You are the sacred life force energy channeling through your body.

Ask yourself, "How does it feel in my body when I remember that I am the awareness behind my thoughts?"

#5
I Am Safe

Fear and trauma cause us to look outside ourselves for safety and for love. But this is how we abandon ourselves and keep ourselves frightened, believing that we are alone. Nothing could be further from the truth.

Hold yourself. Put your arms around yourself and fill the empty wound inside you with love.

Every day tell yourself, "I am safe. I am loved. I got me."

As you develop
your intuition, you
become more
aware of who
you are.

#6
Your Intuition is Part of You

Your intuition is not a gift or an extra "thing" you can develop.

Everything is energy. Energy flows through and around you. Your body is a conduit for energy. It's designed that way.

Intuition is the ability to sense energy. As your consciousness evolves, you become more aware. As you become more aware, your intuition–or ability to sense the energy around you–heightens.

Also as you bring attention to how your intuition works, you become more conscious of who you are as a soul.

What are signs showing you that you are becoming more aware?

To create a new reality, alter the frequency you generate.

#7
Alter Your Frequency

Our thoughts and feelings generate electricity, which creates a frequency. The frequency we generate impacts the physical world and creates our reality.

To create a new reality, we must alter the frequency we generate. The power to do this is in our hands.

Change your thoughts, generate new feelings, and a new world cracks open.

You have the power to create a new reality for yourself.

What thoughts and feelings could you change?

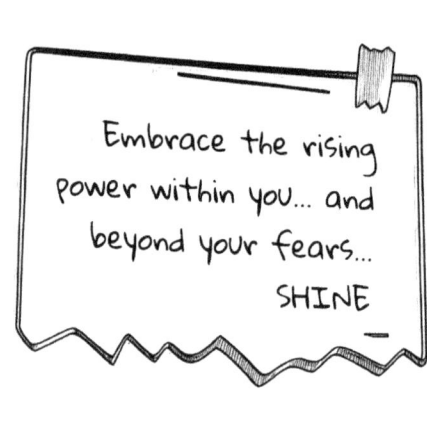

Embrace the rising
power within you... and
beyond your fears...
SHINE

#8
Embrace Your Power

We have been suppressed. And we pushed back. We were pushed down again and we resisted.

We suffered. We rose and fell again and again. For generations.

Healers. Artists. Truth seekers. Communities. Visionaries.

We have done so much work to heal, to release trauma, to find our purpose, and to show up.

Something was bound to happen. It's happening.

The old ways are breaking up. A new power is rising–inside. It might feel unsettling, scary, overwhelming, or exciting.

This new power is yours.

It is more than "yours." It is YOU.

Embrace the rising power within you … and beyond your fears … SHINE

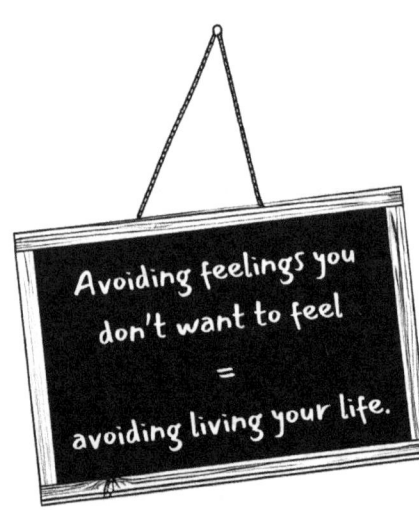

Avoiding feelings you
don't want to feel
=
avoiding living your life.

#9
Live Your Life

You've been misled by your discomforts and your judgements. By avoiding whatever doesn't feel comfortable, you're avoiding living your life.

We seek comfort. There's nothing wrong with that.

Use your inner wisdom to discern, "Am I looking for comfort to avoid dealing with something that would be in my highest good to deal with?"

If you sense the answer is "yes" then trust you are guided to face it. When you sit with uncomfortable feelings and feel them…without reliving the experience…the feelings will resolve and move on.

If the answer is "no" then seek comfort. Tell yourself, "I am safe" and surrender to the feeling of safety and relief.

Where in my life
am I choosing the
"easy path" now,
knowing it may be
harder later?

#10
Challenge Now or Later?

Face your challenges now or later—but you can't escape them.

When you face them now, the path ahead becomes lighter and easier.

When you avoid them, choosing what looks like the easier path, the challenges only wait for you around the corner. Meanwhile, fear follows you as you anticipate their return.

The choice is yours.

Where in my life am I choosing the "easy path" now, knowing it may be harder later?

*You are exactly
where you should be.
Now... expand.*

#11
Be in This Now Moment

You are exactly where you should be. Otherwise you would be somewhere else.

When we think we should be somewhere else, we are not present. We are distracted by thinking about where we are not.

This will leave you feeling ungrounded, confused, and powerless.

Reclaim your power. Be HERE, in this NOW moment.

And... expand your being.

As I continued to
peel open the gifts
of my shadow, I
found it had great
wisdom to share.

#12
Embrace Your Shadow

As I continued to peel open the gifts of my shadow, I found it had great wisdom to share.

As I embraced all of myself, the good and the bad, I began to feel whole and strong, less judgmental of myself and others, more free to speak my truth. A feeling of peace and aliveness permeated my being.

Being spiritual doesn't mean pushing away your shadow. Your shadow is part of you and has wisdom to share.

You might embrace your shadow by holding the frightened part of you to make it feel safe, exploring your wounding to find its source, or by expressing yourself artistically.

Exploring, healing and embracing your shadow can lead you on a path to greater wholeness and wellness.

Is there a part of you that feels weak, frightened, or upset and needs attending to?

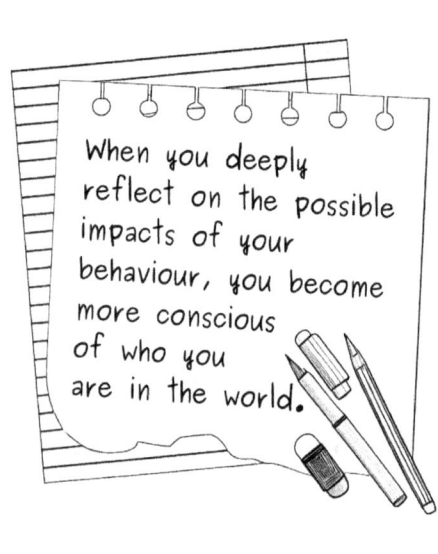

When you deeply
reflect on the possible
impacts of your
behaviour, you become
more conscious
of who you
are in the world.

#13
Impacts You Make

When you deeply reflect on the possible impacts of your behaviour, you become more conscious of who you are in the world, and your ability to relate to others expands.

I remember a time when I spoke with a woman from another culture. I said something that upset her. Initially, I didn't understand. I had good intentions and wanted to connect with her.

Only when I put myself in her shoes could I begin to understand how what I had said had affected her.

I was deeply humbled. I wrote to her to share my insight and apologize. She reached back, moved by what I had shared. Our hearts connected.

It is courageous to reflect on your own behavior and how it impacts others.

Ask your Higher Self, "Where could I put myself in someone else's shoes to understand the impact my words or behavior has had on them?"

And, "What can help me to move from wanting to defend myself, to wanting to understand?"

It was time for me to create a new path and to stop looking for the old one.

#14
Create a New Path

I reflected for a moment. The message was obvious: that it was time for me to create a new path and stop looking for the old one.

This was a time when I was lost in the forest. I tried again and again and again to find the path I had originally taken, but I couldn't find it.

I realized I had to stop looking for the old path. I had to create my own path. I knew where North was and that was the direction I needed to go. From there, I found my way.

Is there somewhere in your life where it's time for you to create a new path? Your path.

#15
Embrace Fear

It's about embracing fear, rather than pushing it away to get rid of it.

Fear is a small wounded part of you that needs to be held, because when you were little and afraid, there was no one there for you.

Trauma was created then. As you go through your life and experience moments similar to when you were younger, old trauma can get triggered again.

Ask your Higher Self, "Where in my life could embracing fear open the door to deeper healing or freedom?"

This is the time to break things open, Not Repeat what you already KNOW.

#16
Open to the New

This is the time to break things open, not repeat what you already know.

Keep opening where it's new, where you don't know, where it is unfamiliar, where you're afraid, where you have anxiety, where you feel ungrounded.

You WILL find your way.

Your intuition is speaking to you all the time. Are you listening?

#17

Your Intuition is Speaking to You

Everything is energy. You are an energy being. Energy flows through everything.

Your body is designed to channel energy.

Intuition is your ability to sense energy. Your intuition is speaking to you all the time. Are you listening?

Practice listening, and it will speak louder and more clearly.

#18
Discern Energy

It is natural that you pick up on energy all the time. This is why discernment is important because not all of it is yours.

Sometimes you might pick up on someone else's headache, bad mood or state of mind. This can be helpful to inform you, but only if you discern it as not yours.

Practice asking yourself, "Is this my energy?" Your inner wisdom already knows the answer.

If it is, then pause and feel it. Let the energy resolve in your body.

If it isn't, then practice saying, "All energy that is not mine, leave now."

You don't need to take on someone else's energy. Use this ability as a source of information about another's wellbeing.

Are you picking up on other people's energy a bit more than usual?

All the work you've
done has been to get
you to *HERE*.

NOW, your real
work begins.

_____
_____
_____

#19
Your Real Work is Now

You have already done a lot of work. The books. The podcasts. The courses. The coaches. The therapists. You have come a long way.

AND all of this work has helped get you HERE, to this point.

It is NOW that your real work begins.

Now is your time to shine.

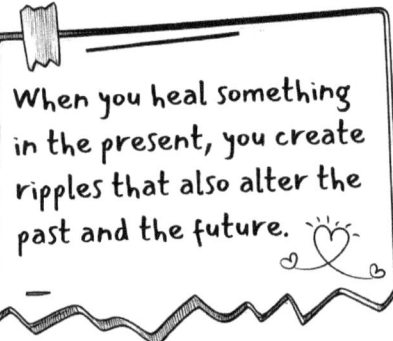

When you heal something in the present, you create ripples that also alter the past and the future.

#20
Heal Past, Present & Future

Your energy is infinite. You are connected with your past and your future.

When you heal something in the present, you create ripples in the energy that also heal the past and the future.

You are that powerful.

Where in your life are you being called to heal at this time? And how could that healing impact your past or your future?

Each time you choose to
open your heart rather
than close it, a brighter
world opens.

#21
Open Your Heart

Each time you choose to open your heart rather than close it, a brighter world opens.

In that moment of choice, towards being open rather than closed, you shift your being to a higher frequency timeline–where things happen that wouldn't have happened otherwise.

Is there somewhere where you could open your heart?

Your opinions separate you. Then you have to justify your opinions by invalidating the "others."

This creates war.

#22
Opinions Separate

There is a lot of noise in the world trying to control your thoughts and beckoning you to have opinions.

Opinions aren't bad. They help you to think.

Opinions also separate. Your opinions separate you when your mind is closed to anything other than your opinion.

When you have an opinion, the mind looks to justify the opinion by invalidating the "others."

This creates war. War can exist in our heart, and in the world. They are the same.

Is there an opinion you're holding to tightly that might be separating you?

*Step out of your mind
and into your heart.*

#23
Move into Your Heart

Many of us grew up in cultures that focused education on the mind and how to think … even what to think.

But thinking is only one way to access information and understanding.

Our head brain has been burdened with the responsibility of figuring it all out. That was never meant to be.

Your heart center can also be called a brain. According to some research, it generates an electromagnetic field that is at least 100 times stronger than that generated by the head brain. Your heart is the doorway to a greater intelligence beyond your thinking mind. It is also the home of compassion and connection with yourself and with others.

Step out of your mind and into your heart … where your real world exists.

Are you trying to "think" things through too much rather than listening to the wisdom of your heart?

Let go of what
you know –
to REMEMBER
who you are.

#24
Let Go to Remember

Let go of what you know–to REMEMBER who you are.

When you decide you know yourself, you close the door to seeing yourself in a new way.

And when you act "beyond" the character you know, in a good way or a bad way, you might say, "I wasn't being myself. I was acting out of character."

In this way we keep ourselves in "known" boxes of judgements and expectations limiting our ways of being.

In order to REMEMBER who you really are, you must let go of what you know… and allow yourself to BECOME…

Whatever you choose these circumstances to mean... creates the path before you.

#25
Your Interpretation Creates Your World

Your brain automatically interprets the world around you. But what guides it to decipher your circumstances are the beliefs you already hold.

If you hold beliefs of lack and aggression, then you will perceive your circumstances through these lenses.

If you hold beliefs of generosity and good will, that is how you will "see" the same circumstances.

You are not a victim to your beliefs. You can change them … consciously.

There is no absolute "reality" that only has one truth.

Whatever you choose your circumstances to mean … creates the path before you.

Could you benefit from changing how you interpret your circumstances?

When you listen to your inner wisdom, you reconnect with Source inside you - then no one can tell you what to believe, what to do, or what is true.

#26
Reconnect with Source

Many of us grew up being taught to obey external authority and ignore our own inner guidance system.

This causes separation within the Self.

But when you begin to listen to your inner senses, to what feels right to you at an intuitive level, you reconnect with Source inside you. That is how you find your way back home and back to your own wisdom.

When you access your own inner wisdom, no one can tell you what to believe, what to do, or what is true … because you can feel it for yourself … beyond fear.

What are your senses telling you right now?

Put your fears and insecurities in the back seat where they feel safe — and you take the steering wheel.

#27
Make Your Fears Feel Safe

Your fears, doubts, and insecurities took shape as you grew up. They provided lenses for you to view the world and to learn. This helped you to grow.

As you realize that you've been letting them run your life, the wise adult you steps in to take charge. You put them in the back seat, where they feel safe, and you take the steering wheel.

Is there somewhere in your life where the wise adult you needs to step in?

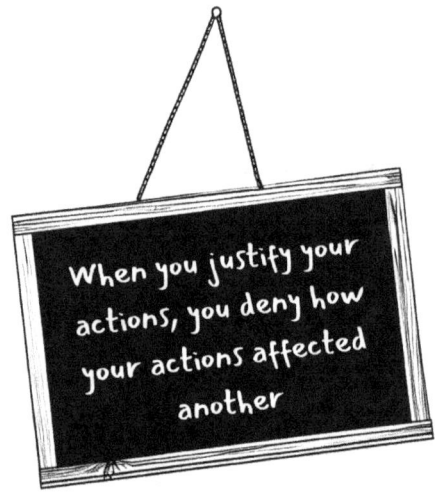

When you justify your actions, you deny how your actions affected another

and invalidate their feelings.

#28
When You Justify

When you justify your actions and say you didn't intend to have a negative impact, you deny the reality of how your actions have affected others, and you invalidate their feelings.

You make it more difficult for your apology to be heard.

When someone feels hurt by your actions, it does not mean that you intended to hurt them or that you are a bad person.

It simply means that the other person got hurt.

When you take time to understand why they felt hurt, and really listen…your heart can open allowing the hurt in both of you to resolve. You are that powerful.

Is there somewhere where you could reach to understand why someone else feels hurt and bring forth this kind of power?

Developing intuition...

is a journey of bringing
mindful attention to what
your senses are picking up
and trusting what
you are sensing.

#29
Develop Your Intuition

Developing your intuition is actually very easy and simple.

Given that everything is energy, your intuition is your ability to "pick up" on and sense energy. Energy in the field. Energy around you. Energy flowing through you.

Developing your intuition is a journey of bringing mindful attention to what your senses are picking up and trusting what you are sensing.

Is there a choice you need to make in your life that would benefit from you sensing more into your intuition for clarity?

#30
Overwhelm is Optional

Overwhelm is caused by getting stuck in your head and allowing past trauma to tell you, "I can't handle this."

When we were little, if we were exposed to situations we didn't have the inner resources or support to process, this may have caused trauma.

Habits of thinking can get established such as, "I'm all alone" and "I can't do this."

As an adult, when a lot is going on and we want to expand beyond our current state of consciousness, this old trauma can become reactive.

The traumatized mind wants to slow things down or stop everything until things settle.

It's the wise adult you who can step in to speak to the trauma-triggered little you and say, "I am here. It isn't your job to handle this. I'm going to do that."

Breathe deeply and slowly to regulate your nervous system, as you take one step into the unknown expansion of yourself.

Overwhelm is optional. Be there for yourself as you expand your capacity.

You are the awareness
in which all of life
appears. You are truly
divine.

#31
You Are Divine

The reality of who you are is far greater than you can see in the mirror.

You are not your face. You are not your body. You are not the thoughts in your mind.

We find it difficult to fathom the truth of who we are because our thinking blinds us. It distracts us with thoughts such as, "I'm not good enough. I don't matter. I'm not loved."

But the truth is–we are consciousness channeling through a body. We are the awareness in which all of life appears.

Summarized from some of the main spiritual teachings—we are the timeless essence many call soul, spirit, or pure consciousness.

Who we are is truly divine.

Imagine yourself outside of the present reality you observe, with no constraints or limits. How do you feel?

The moment you compromise yourself, problems will follow.

#32
Compromise

Many people believe that they have to compromise themselves in relationships, but this is not true.

Negotiation and agreement are necessary, but the moment you compromise yourself, problems will follow.

When you compromise, you give away something that is important to you. In the immediate, you might tell yourself that it doesn't matter.

Over time, resentment and unhappiness builds.

Is there somewhere in your life where you are about to compromise yourself?

#33
Your Intuition Tells You What Feels Right

When you access your intuition, it's easier to be YOU.

It's easier to know when to speak or take action and when to be still and observe.

When you are actively working with your intuition, you are paying attention to what "feels" right and what doesn't.

You can "sense" and discern more easily when to move and where to go.

Your intuition is part of your senses. You have outer senses in your body and you have inner senses. It is a natural part of you that helps you to have a broader and deeper perspective on the world around you and inside of you.

Bring more awareness to what "feels" right and what doesn't feel right to you. Be guided by that.

Become unwilling to hold on to who you are not.

#34
Let Go of Who You Are Not

This is how you expand who you are––when you're unwilling to hold on to who you are not.

When you refuse to keep believing the limiting thoughts that hold you back and keep you small, it follows naturally that your being expands.

You become clear and focused in your intentions rather than preoccupied with attending to wounds that are perpetuated by limiting thoughts of not being enough.

You are a Divine Being. Keep letting go of who you are not.

Dream your
dreams.

Declare your
intentions.

Face your fears and
walk, run, dance, fly,
wise one.

#35
Face Your Fears and Fly

Dream your dreams. Declare your intentions. Face your fears and walk, run, dance, fly, wise one.

This is what you came here for. To live and to experience life.

Face your fears and allow them to resolve in your body, your heart, and your soul.

You are free.

Fly.

The moment you declare it to be, it is so.

#36
Declaration

Our words are energy that carry a pattern and a frequency. This frequency impacts the physical.

For example, singing and chanting can take the body and mind into an altered state.

When you gain clarity and declare with certainty, "It is done," the energy and frequency of that clarity and the words you say begin shaping your reality.

The moment you declare it to be, it is so.

Is there something you are getting ready to declare? Either to declare the "end of" or the "beginning of" or something new?

When we attend to our own needs, we don't have to fight to get them met.

#37
Meet Your Needs

This is not about being self-reliant or about not needing anyone.

Being with others is one of our needs. We are meant to connect with one another.

But when we look to others to fulfill our needs, it's a sign that we are not in right relationship with our Self.

As in any relationship that you want to build and sustain, a relationship with your Self requires being kind, loving and respectful, honoring your promises, and nourishing yourself with care and good food.

When your relationship with your Self is strong, you are aware of your needs, and you ensure they are attended to.

When we attend to our own needs, we don't have to fight to get them met.

And when your needs are met… you have an abundance of love and generosity to share.

Where could you be attending to your Self with more love?

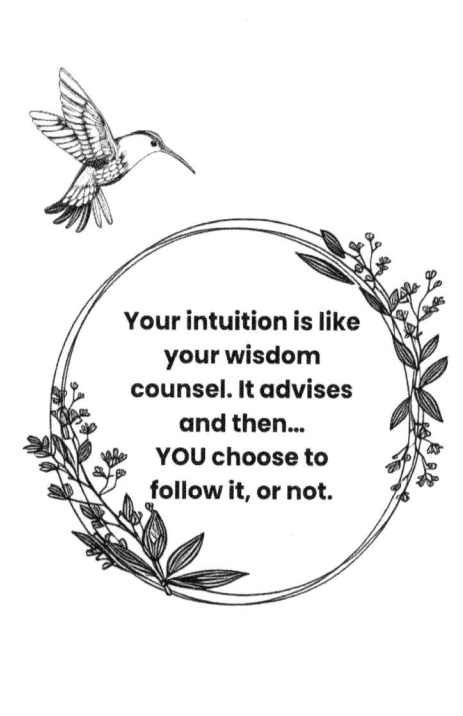

Your intuition is like
your wisdom
counsel. It advises
and then...
YOU choose to
follow it, or not.

#38

You Are Not Victim to Your Intuition

Your inner wisdom doesn't take responsibility for your life. It's the flow of spirit through you, which you're tapping into.

Your intuition never tells you what to do. And you are not a victim of your intuition.

Your intuition is like your wisdom counsel. It advises you and then…

YOU choose to follow it. Or not.

Sometimes resistance can arise when we receive an intuitive message that we don't like. Maybe it is challenging us to expand beyond our comfort zone or to face something we don't want to face.

Are you sensing an intuitive message that might be challenging for you to receive?

Remember you have a choice.

It takes a lot of
courage to pause and
be honest with yourself.

#39
Be Honest with Yourself

It takes a lot of courage to pause and be honest with yourself.

To stop and look into your eyes in the mirror.

To stick your head in the well of your insides and face what is there. To listen deeply to the truth in your heart.

[Quote from my book: *Real & Wild You*]

Maybe your heart has something to tell you that you need to hear.

#40
Let Your Inner Wisdom Guide You

Upon returning from my steep hill climb, I couldn't find my special walking stick, which I had hidden behind a fallen tree for safe keeping.

As I looked further, I realized there were hundreds of fallen trees and branches. My staff could be behind any of them.

I closed my eyes and slowed my breath. Holding in my mind the image of my stick, I sent out a telepathic call to help me find it.

I opened my eyes and paid attention. I moved wherever I felt "guided" to move. I found my stick within moments.

[Quote from my book: *Real & Wild You*]

Stop trying to figure it all out with your head. Work with your inner wisdom to guide you.

You being in your joy
makes a difference in
the world. This is
who you are.

#41
You Are Joy

Joy is simply being you. By being yourself and experiencing joy, you attract amazing experiences into your life.

Joy is different from "having fun."

Joy is something that makes your soul sing. It uplifts you. You being in your joy makes a difference in the world.

It makes you want to shine, and to shine brighter.

This is who you are.

Follow your joy.

When you choose to think
different thoughts...
a doorway opens
to a new
reality.

#42
Choose Different Thoughts

Your thoughts create the reality you see. If you think that there is abundance, you see abundance.

If you think that there is scarcity, you see scarcity.

Most of your thoughts are habitual, which means you create the same reality each day.

But when you CHOOSE to think different thoughts… a doorway opens to a new reality.

Can you identify the thoughts you have that create a reality you don't want?

What might happen if you choose to think and act beyond your habitual patterns?

Your ego will always tell you you're separate and on your own. But that isn't truth. ‼⁉

#43
You Are Always Connected

Your ego will always tell you you're separate and on your own.

When you do the work to heal and open your heart, you reconnect with your Self.

It's like electricity. When a wire has been severed, it can't connect. And when the wire is "healed" it reconnects.

When your heart is open, you feel the connection. With yourself. With others. With the all.

That's reality. That's the truth.

Feel your heart … open … and connected.

Love is a powerful place
inside yourself. And
when you are present in
that love — anything
that is not love —
dissolves.

#44
Power of Love

Love doesn't mean... all nice and fluffy and pink.

Sometimes love is tough. Love can have you on the edge saying something hard to somebody you care about. Risking everything... to try and restore love.

That's love.

Love is about holding the space for LOVE to show up and be there. You might do this through kindness, generosity, and caring, or by speaking out or challenging someone you love.

Love is a powerful place inside yourself. When you are present in that love, anything that is not love dissolves.

Where could you bring more love?

Let go and trust
whatever unfolds...
is in the highest
good for all.

#45
Let Go and Trust

I had made it, and in a couple of hours, the course would begin.

I stomped each foot to feel the soles of my feet on the ground. This was real. I closed my eyes as they welled with tears of gratitude.

Grateful for all the miracles that had conspired, and for the courage it had taken me to find myself standing here—from buying my ticket, to listening to my intuition, leaving my bag behind, and making my flight. I breathed in deeply.

I am here.

[Quote from my book: *Open Me*]

When you let go into what seems impossible and follow the guidance of a greater consciousness, miracles can happen.

You can't make miracles happen or force your agenda. You have to let go and trust that whatever unfolds…is for the highest good of all.

Is your ego-mind holding
you back from stepping
into a greater possibility?

#46
Break the Habit of Your Ego

Your ego keeps you small.

But remember, your ego isn't bad. It's just a collection of habitual thoughts/beliefs from the past.

Beliefs about who you are, what's possible and not possible for you. Beliefs about the world and your relationship to others.

These thoughts repeat themselves and have been for as long as you have had these beliefs.

Your ego is a habit, repeatedly telling you who you are supposed to be. Nothing more.

You know how to break habits.

Is your ego-mind holding you back from stepping into a greater possibility?

A calling is the flow of
spirit encouraging you
to go one way,
or to go
another
way.

#47
A Calling

With a question in my mind, I felt myself drawn to stray from the path. It led me to a river I didn't know was there.

Kneeling down to touch the cool water, I asked, "What is a calling?"

As I watched the water flow freely, I received its message. "A calling is the flow of spirit encouraging you to go one way, or to go another way."

[Quote from my book: *Real & Wild You*]

Maybe you are feeling a "calling" towards something.

Pay attention to the nudges you might feel that are trying to guide you.

As we heal our relationship with our Self, and with each other... bit by bit we are coming home.

#48
Heal Relationships

We were brought up in a culture with an ethos of competition, dominance, suppression of the feminine, and invalidation of intuition.

This tore us apart inside and damaged our connection to each other.

As you heal your relationship with your Self and with others…bit by bit you come home to your wholeness.

How could you bring more care to your relationship with yourself and others?

Your strength lies in the unknown, in the illogical, irrational and impossible.

Look there.

#49
Beyond the Limits of the Mind

Your strength lies in the unknown, in the illogical, irrational and impossible.

Look there.

When you step beyond who you think you are–into the space of not knowing how you will do this–you access a greater part of you.

Our mind will always impose limits. That is how it works. By habit.

But when you push beyond those limits, new abilities show up, and dormant gifts step in.

A next level you arises.

How would you show up differently if you allowed yourself to step into the unknown, the illogical, irrational and what seems impossible in your life?

When you open your

heart and be authentic

and vulnerable, this is

where your real power is.

#50
Vulnerability and Strength

When we gloss over the truth of deeper feelings by saying, "I'm fine," "Everything's okay," "It's all good" …we diminish ourselves by hiding.

When you open your heart and be authentic and vulnerable, this is where your real power is.

Being honest and vulnerable is what heals. This is where love lives.

How would it feel to be more vulnerable and open?

Step into the unknown
with an inner trust
that everything will
turn out okay, no
matter what
happens.

#51
Step into the Unknown

Step into the unknown with an inner trust that everything will turn out okay, no matter what happens.

There is so much noise fighting for your attention—telling you what is right and wrong, true and false, what to think, how to be. It's deafening.

It can be challenging to listen to your own inner wisdom…and to TRUST yourself.

It might feel as if you are stepping into the unknown blindly, and maybe that's a good thing. It means you can create something that's never been created before.

Trust. Keep doing the work to listen to your inner wisdom, and keep taking one step after another.

Keep going. You are on track.

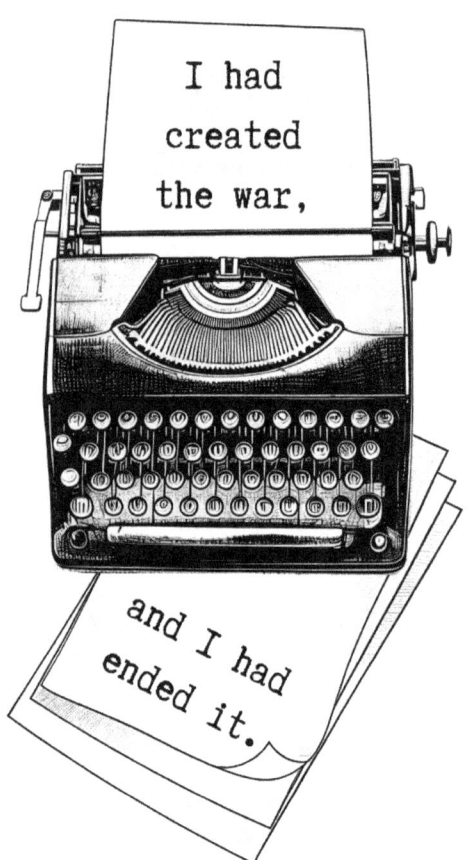

I had
created
the war,

and I had
ended it.

#52
End the War Inside

At some point during one of the exercises, after I had used up a whole box of tissues crying about something, the thing I was crying about suddenly seemed completely trivial.

I had gone to the bottom of the barrel. There was nowhere else to go. And now being at the bottom didn't seem so bad.

I stopped crying. There was peace in my heart.

It was as if there had been a war going on inside me, and all of a sudden it stopped. I saw how much drama and significance I had generated around things that now seemed hardly to matter at all.

I had created the war, and I had ended it.

The circumstances I had been so upset about still existed. But I was no longer at war inside myself.

[Quote from my book: *Open Me*]

There are many things to be upset about in the world. But the "war" inside only perpetuates problems.

The way out is through your own pain. Sit with it. Feel it. Let it resolve … until it's gone. End the war inside you.

Your being matters.

The effort to interrupt
self sabotaging
thoughts and actions is
an act of self love.

#53
Act of Self Love

As we grow up on this beautiful planet of "hard knocks," we experience. We learn.

We form beliefs about ourselves. Some of them are unhelpful, such as: I'm not enough. I don't matter. I don't deserve. I don't belong.

Sometimes we even learn to not like ourselves. When this happens, we can develop a habit of sabotaging ourselves.

We won't let ourselves have the things we want, because we believe we are unworthy.

When you make the effort to interrupt self sabotaging thoughts and actions, you've taken the first step to loving yourself and breaking this cycle.

Any effort to interrupt self-sabotage is an act of self love.

You might have to interrupt your self sabotaging patterns again and again. But you are worth it. Right?

Pick one, small self sabotaging thought or action to interrupt. Focus only on breaking that one. Do it for one week. Then decide if you'll do it for another week.

You are unstoppable.

Fulfilment is the journey regardless of what is happening.

#54
Fulfilment

Fulfilment is the journey regardless of what is happening.

Many people look for fulfilment as if it has something to do with outer circumstances or with getting somewhere.

But these things won't bring you fulfilment.

I have found that being fulfilled is never about getting things or being somewhere or having everything perfect.

It's about having a heart that can hold everything that is happening–without resisting any of it.

When you open your heart to hold everything with no resistance … in that embrace … is love, compassion, and joy.

That's fulfilment.

How much love can you hold in your heart?

I feel more authentic as
I begin to have more
honest conversations
with others.

#55
Be Authentic

When I drop the mask and the pretense and instead be honest, and in my heart, in conversation with others, I feel more authentic.

It's actually a relief. I'm more grounded and present.

Any interaction is much more enjoyable.

Can you drop the mask and the pretense, and be in your heart, all day today?

One morning, as I lay in bed feeling sorry for myself, I did the one thing I hadn't thought of.

I asked for help.

#56
Ask for Help

One morning, as I lay in bed feeling sorry for myself, I did the one thing I hadn't thought of.

I asked for help.

Closing my eyes, I whispered, "Dear Creator and all the master souls working with me, I need your help."

A soothing calmness entered my heart and surrounded me. I felt like I was being held. I had been so lost in my own terror that I had forgotten I wasn't alone.

[Quote from my book: *Open Me*]

Are you trying to go it alone without asking for help?

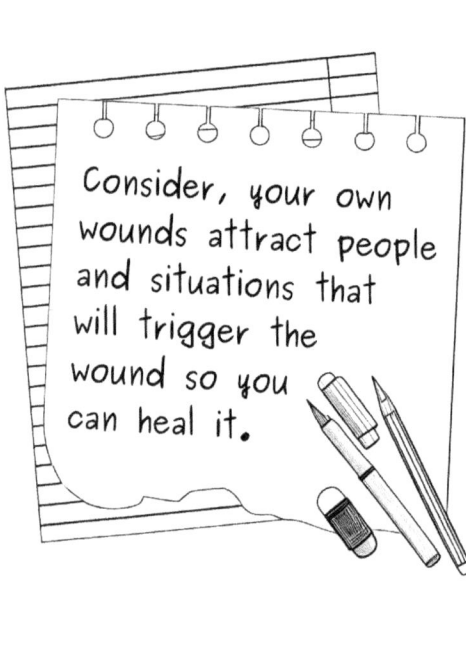

Consider, your own wounds attract people and situations that will trigger the wound so you can heal it.

#57
Open More to Love

You attract people and situations that will trigger your wounds so you can heal them.

Your body and soul want to be whole because YOU are LOVE.

Anything that is not love within you has to be resolved.

Attracting people and circumstances that highlight your wounds is a blessing and an invitation for you to continue opening to love.

Where could you open more to love?

Guide your cells in
better habits. You are
the master and guardian
of your body.

#58
Teach Your Cells Better Habits

The ego-mind and the body crave the fixes: food, drink, sleep, or distraction–because your cells have been trained in these habits.

Your body is simply doing what it has learned from you. You are not a victim to your body. You trained it.

As you grew up and figured things out, you consciously or unconsciously made decisions about what works and what doesn't.

Your cells followed your lead.

Your cells don't know the difference between a "good" habit and a "bad" one. But you do. You are the one who decides.

Now that you are more aware of this, you can retrain your body differently.

What is one unhelpful pattern my body follows that no longer serves me, and how could I retrain it differently?

Open yourself and let yourself be supported by others.

#59
Be Supported

My mother took my face in her hands like only a mother can. She looked into my eyes. "Oh honey, it hurts doesn't it?" she said gently.

She didn't know what I was sad about. She just felt my sadness and acknowledged it. That was all I needed.

A depth of grief that I didn't even know was there spilled out of me with the tears. I was sad about my marriage, sad about losing friends, sad about leaving the farm.

I was sad about an old lover, sad about my dad. I was sad that I hadn't let my mom hold me like this before.

My mother held me while I sobbed, and I let her. I didn't pull away. There was no more resistance inside me.

Only love.

[Quote from my book: *Open Me*]

Open yourself and let yourself be supported by others.

#60
Be True to You

When you feel you've been true to yourself, you feel good about who you are.

When you deliver on the promises you make to yourself…

When you interrupt your thoughts from speaking unkindly about yourself…

When you treat yourself with caring and kindness…

When you don't hold back where you usually do…

When you respect your boundaries…

These are moments of being true to yourself. When you do these things, you build a stronger relationship with yourself and naturally feel good about who you are.

In a culture where being true to yourself isn't valued…it is a revolutionary act to be true to yourself.

Where can you be more true to yourself? Can you invite someone else into this revolutionary act along with you?

**Listen to your heart.
It will always guide
you to the right
place.**

#61
Listen to Your Heart

*I let myself sit and really feel what my heart had said.
"I want to live like this."*

*Like a pot of tea, I let it seep, allowing the true flavours
of every leaf, flower, and root to release their messages
into the water.*

*As the message seeped into me, I realised that I longed
to live in nature and take the time for moments of quiet
and solitude, just like I was doing then.*

*This desire had been deeply buried under my belief
that in order to succeed, I had to work hard, and that I
didn't have time for moments like this.*

[Quote from my book: *Open Me*]

Carve out time and space to listen to your heart. It
will always guide you to the right place.

Love.

And let go.

#62
Love and Let Go

You were born love. You still are love. Loving is your natural state.

Your heart naturally wants to give and to connect with others.

It's only from wounding that we close our hearts and become conditional with our love. "I'll give if you give."

This isn't love. This is trade and an attempt to get our needs met.

It creates obligation, resentment and upset.

When you love, if you are looking for any response from the other, then the love you are giving is conditional.

Can you give love with no conditions, no expectations, no hope of response?

Love. And let go.

Expressing yourself in
the world from your
uplifted feelings is
your purpose.

#63
Your Purpose

Sometimes we can get caught thinking, "I don't know what my purpose is. What is my purpose?"

We go looking for our purpose outside ourselves…in courses, books, gurus…hoping someone will tell us.

But searching for your purpose will have you forever chasing your tail.

Some people think their purpose is a tangible thing, like reaching a certain goal or living a particular kind of lifestyle.

Your purpose is simpler than you think. Because it's already inside you. It's connected with whatever uplifts you, brings you joy, feeds your spirit.

When you are in these good feelings, your purpose is how you express yourself in the world.

Pay attention to what uplifts you and what does not. Just because you are good at something, does not mean it is your purpose.

Expressing yourself in the world from your uplifted feelings is your purpose.

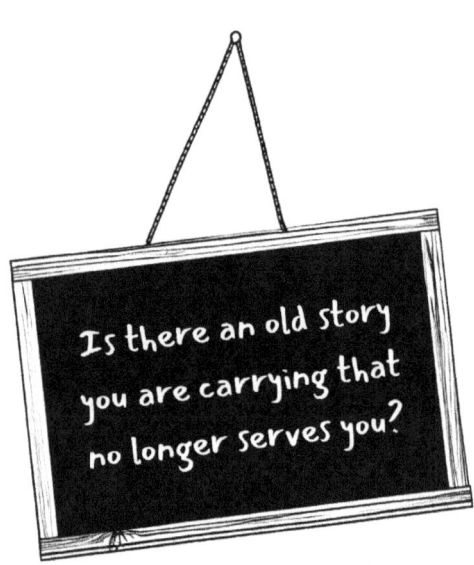

Is there an old story you are carrying that no longer serves you?

#64
Old Stories to Put Down

When my marriage broke up, I experienced a lot of hurt. Sure it takes two, but he did hurtful things, I had a right to feel hurt, and it was his fault that I felt so hurt. Right?

Emotional wounding can happen in relationships when other people (parents, children, friends, spouses, siblings, bosses) do not fulfil our expectations or desires and we blame them.

Of course I had every right to feel hurt. I have a right to feel whatever I feel. It is healthy to feel and to let those feelings flow ... But in a healthy way.

When I handle those feelings in unhealthy ways such as lashing out, blaming others or continuing to recount the story of what happened and how I was hurt, this wounds me again and it wounds those around me.

[Quote from my book: *Real & Wild You*]

Is there an old story you are carrying that no longer serves you?

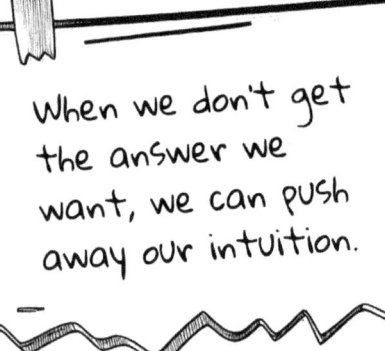

When we don't get the answer we want, we can push away our intuition.

#65
Blaming Your Intuition

How strange to have faced so many challenges, not to mention an angry spirit from a past life, only to find myself now sitting in what felt like the Garden of Eden having all my wishes granted.

When I first arrived in Malta, I thought that the angels had left me. But it was actually me who had left them. It was me who had stopped listening.

It was only when I'd had enough of my own misery that I started to listen to my intuition again. Had my journey ended at this moment as I sat in this Garden of Eden, I would have been completely satisfied. But it wasn't over yet.

[Quote from my book: *Open Me*]

Sometimes when circumstances don't go the way we want them to, we can blame our intuition for not giving us the right answers.

We might even ignore our intuition and go back into the ego-mind to try to get what we want.

This never goes well, and only repeats the past.

Where could you let go to trust again?

The moment I compromised, I lost my heart, my spirit, myself.

#66
Negotiate

I had compromised myself so many times, and each time I was trying to hang on to something I was afraid of losing.

But the moment I compromised, I lost anyway. I lost my heart. I lost my spirit. I lost trust. I lost myself.

[Quote from my book: *Real & Wild You*]

Are you in a situation where you think you have to give up something that is important to you?

Get clear on what is important to you and what is non-negotiable. Then negotiate.

Trust you will find a way forward.

whatever is
happening
IS
the journey.

#67
This is the Journey

I sat on a bench to assess my situation, and taking a nice, deep breath, I decided something that would greatly impact the rest of my travels: whatever happened on my journey WAS the journey.

[Quote from my book: *Open Me*]

When we have a plan about how we want something to go and things happen differently than we planned, we might regard this as a detour or something that wasn't supposed to happen.

This can cause upset, and it is where "we" detour from the flow of the universe.

When we embrace what is happening in each moment, whether desired, expected or not–we are more in touch with the opportunity of each moment.

And we are flowing with the current of life and are more connected with our intuition.

Whatever is happening IS the journey.

Our natural way
of being is love.

#68
Love is Natural

Our natural way of being is love.

That's why it takes so much energy to be angry, sad, and resentful–lashing out at others–because you're going against the current of who you are.

That's exhausting. It's exhausting to keep yourself suppressed.

This explains why, when you relax and let go of muscle tension, your heart opens and you begin to feel a flow of love.

Love is the NATURAL flow of energy through your body. Only YOU can stop it. Only YOU can let it flow.

Let it flow, baby.

#69
Threshold of Commitment

"I'll help you with your book if you write it," she said.

I sat there blinking and looked down at the ground while her words bounced around in my head: "If" I write it. Am I going to write it?

Thinking about writing a book and actually writing it were two different worlds. I swallowed and closed my eyes. I was scared.

What if it's a flop? What if I quit before it's done? What if it's just too hard? What if I spend all that time and money for nothing? What if I prove to myself and everyone else that I really am a failure?

I moved my awareness into my heart and began breathing slowly and deeply into the centre of my chest. My heartbeat was strong and steady.

I asked my heart if it wanted to write a book. As I asked this question, my heart seemed to open more, and I felt excited. I sensed that my heart had been waiting for this.

I looked up at the morning sun shining through the trees and said, "I will."

[Quote from my book: *Real & Wild You*]

Is there something in your heart that is waiting for you to say, "I will"?

Perfectionism can be a form of self-abuse because you keep pushing away the feeling of satisfaction in what you've created.

#70
Perfectionism

The habitual pattern of perfectionism can be a killer. It can have you forever invalidating what you create.

Perfectionism can be a form of self-abuse, because you keep pushing away the feeling of satisfaction in what you've created.

In a sense, you hold yourself back from having what you want by telling yourself whatever you create "isn't good enough." In this way, you avoid the responsibility that comes from actually having it.

Where could you embrace what you've created in a way that uplifts you?

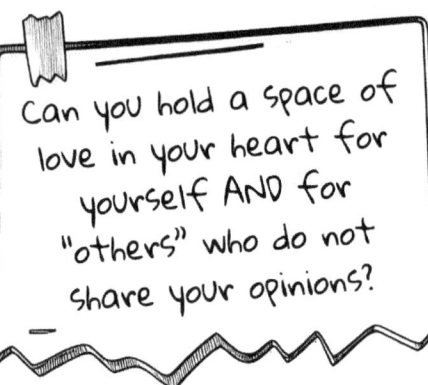

Can you hold a space of love in your heart for yourself AND for "others" who do not share your opinions?

#71
Love for "Others"

We can often try to convince others to agree with our opinions. But this doesn't always go very well and can create division. It doesn't have to be this way.

When you stop trying to convince others, it does not mean you have to agree or accept their opinions.

Opinions are like colors. Can you be with two different colors existing side by side?

When you hold a space of love in your heart for yourself and for others, who hold varied opinions from yours–it means that YOU are a force of love.

You don't have to do anything with their opinion. Nothing needs to be forced or fixed.

In that space of love, things will resolve. Not by your agenda. Not by anyone's agenda–but love's.

Isn't that what you came here for?

Can you hold a space of love in your heart for yourself AND for "others" who do not share your opinions?

#72
You Are Further Than You Think

Be patient with yourself. You are so much further than you think.

We can get so busy thinking of where we want to go and how much more we have to accomplish ... that we lose sight of how far we have come.

Every tiny shift you have made has contributed to something bigger. Every small thing you did, was actually a BIG thing.

If you stand back and reflect on where you started, you are so much further than you realize ... in so many ways.

Let go of trying to control. Let yourself break... into the vastness of YOU.

#73
Let Go of Control

Let go of trying to control. Let yourself break...
into the vastness of YOU.

It's the ego-mind that tries to control the expansiveness of this present moment because it wants to understand, analyse and figure out how to handle it.

This can cause a lot of stress and anxiety.

It tries to shove things into files and boxes of already known information in your brain.

The ego-mind can invalidate the moment into smallness.

When you let go of trying to control, it might seem scary at first because you are interrupting the ego-mind, but as you keep letting go ... you tap into your greater consciousness and the vastness of YOU.

Each time you rise,
you return more
whole.

#74
Rise Again

On this human journey, you will fall again and again.

You'll take wrong turns, break promises, and face the weight of opinions, judgments, and conditioning that try to keep you small.

Your conditioning has taught you that falling means you are weak and bad.

Yet each time YOU RISE, you break free a little more.

Each time you get up, you are more whole.

This is the process of transformation. It is an ongoing evolution into your wholeness.

Are you on the rise?

Your soul whispers its desires to your heart.

#75
Your Soul's Desires

Your soul whispers its desires to your heart. Your heart knows what you really want.

Your desires don't live in your head. Your head holds information like a filing cabinet.

When we use only our head to make decisions, we limit what is possible and often repeat the past. We are not intune with our soul's desires.

But when the head brain is not burdened with making decisions on its own, it has space to get creative with new ideas.

When you work together with your heart and your head to make decisions, you're guided by your soul's desires. You might discover more synchronicities and ease.

But start with your heart. From there, everything else falls into place. What does your heart really want?

Your body and all of its habits are going to live your life, or YOU are.

#76
Habits Living Your Life?

Either your body and all of its habits are going to live your life, or YOU are.

Your body learns habits: how you digest food, how you hold yourself in movement or stillness, even how you think.

The brain, too, runs on habit. Some studies show that over 90% of the thoughts we think each day are the same as the day before.

Without conscious attention, your body and mind slip into autopilot and run without you.

Your body and your automatic thoughts can live your life for you … or YOU can.

How can you practice being more embodied rather than running on autopilot? How present can you be?

#77
Loving Yourself Leads to Peace

All issues, upsets, and problems in your life are caused by you not being in right relationship with yourself.

You learn to not trust yourself each time you: compromise on what's important to you (say "yes" when you mean "no"), don't listen to what your heart is trying to tell you, or don't deliver on the promises you made to yourself.

When you do these things, it leaves you feeling conflicted inside, disappointed, frustrated, resentful, and unhappy with yourself.

This leads to problems.

When you begin healing your relationship and restoring your integrity with yourself, you will find more peace inside.

The peace was always there.

What is one thing you could do towards healing your relationship with your Self and restoring your integrity with You?

When you are honest
with yourself, all
discomfort dissolves.

#78
Be Honest with Yourself

We often don't realize how painful it is to keep breaking our promises to ourselves.

When we fall out of integrity with ourselves, we end up lying just to make ourselves feel more comfortable.

But those lies only create deeper discomfort. Then to avoid that discomfort, we avoid sitting in stillness.

The moment we're willing to be honest, to admit where we've deceived ourselves, all discomfort dissolves.

If you were to be radically honest with yourself right now, what would you admit to yourself and what discomfort might that resolve?

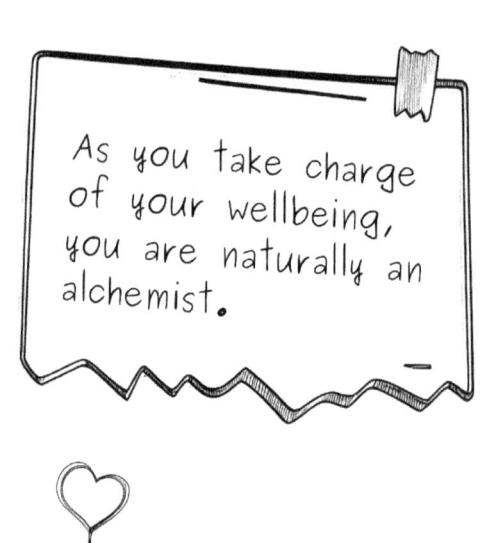

As you take charge
of your wellbeing,
you are naturally an
alchemist.

#79
You Are an Alchemist

Your body is biochemical, which means that all of its processes are run by chemical reactions.

Your thoughts and emotions create chemistry. You could say that this chemistry feeds your body.

If you want a healthier body, or to raise the frequency of energy in your body, you can change the chemistry that runs it by changing your thoughts and feelings.

By generating more positive thinking and more uplifting feelings, you are performing alchemy.

As you take charge of your wellbeing, you are naturally an alchemist.

How could you alter your thoughts in this moment to uplift you?

Your thoughts shape your reality.

#80
Your Thoughts Create Your Reality

Your thoughts shape your reality. But where do those thoughts come from? Are they just random, and you're a victim to them, or are you making them happen?

Are your thoughts automatic? Are you regurgitating an old story? Are your thoughts filled with opinions and judgments making commentary on everything you see?

Consider that these thoughts aren't YOU. The conscious, wise YOU doesn't need to repeat useless thoughts or have unkind judgements about others.

These automatic thoughts are triggered by the brain…and the problem is YOU are listening to them.

That's like listening to the radio tell you what to think and what to do.

Instead of reacting to your thoughts, what happens when you pause and observe them?

#81
You Already Know

You can sometimes feel adrift when you're not listening to your own inner wisdom (also known as intuition).

Your intuition is always communicating with you, whether you are aware of it or not.

And when you are not listening, you are more susceptible to letting others influence what you decide to do.

But the truth is, you already know the answer deep inside.

#82
Beyond What You Know

Where does your logic come from? Your logic comes from what you already know and the logical prediction of repeated patterns.

When you do research, you simply add to your database of knowledge, which then becomes part of what you already know.

But your logic cannot take into account the vastness of this present moment.

This present moment is filled with things you don't know. The next moment will be too. Therefore, the present and future are also filled with opportunities you can't plan for from your logical mind.

If you use only your logic, it's going to follow a known pattern and not be open to the ever-changing landscape of new opportunities that can arise.

Use your logic to inform you and your intuition to guide you beyond what you know.

Where could you step beyond the limits of what you already know?

Every attempt weakens the habit - the only true failure is in giving up.

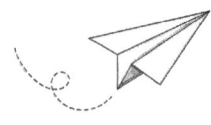

#83
Perseverance to Break Habits

You won't break an old habit, or implement a new one, if you give up after your first failed attempt. In fact, "giving up" might itself be an old habit you want to break.

If you feel like giving up, make perseverance part of your challenge to break through.

[Quote from my book: *Real & Wild You*]

When you are breaking an old habit, it might take many failed attempts before it works.

Each time you attempt to break the habit, you weaken it. There is no failure in the ongoing attempt to break it.

The only failure is in giving up.

Is there something you were about to give up on?

It takes courage to
follow the wisdom
of your soul.

#84
You Are Courageous

It takes courage to follow the wisdom of your soul.

There are many influences impacting your every thought, feeling, and action. The culture we grew up in. Societal expectations. Education. Political narratives. Media. Entertainment.

Your intuition does not follow any rules. It's informed by the wisdom of your soul and knows what is for your highest good.

Following the wisdom of your soul often means creating your own path, listening to your inner compass and not the outer noise.

This takes courage. It's a good thing that's what you've got.

The more you nurture the relationship with yourself, the more stable and whole you feel.

#85
Nurture Your Relationship with You

When you heal your relationship with yourself by keeping your promises to you and truly caring for you, you naturally grow stronger inside.

This inner strength grounds you and sharpens your focus.

You realize that all feelings of instability come from being disconnected with yourself.

The more you nurture your relationship with yourself, the more stable and whole you will feel.

When you feel more stable and whole, this impacts everything in your life.

Where could you strengthen your relationship with yourself?

Nature is speaking to us
all the time. Pause to
connect.

#86
Connect with Nature

Beginning my morning walk, I stepped out onto the street. My mind full. Big plans. Big move.

Taking in a deep breath I closed my eyes and let out a long sigh. "Give me a sign," I whispered.

When I opened my eyes and lifted my head, I gasped and froze.

There in the sky, shaped by the clouds, was a massive eagle head. Not in profile. But staring at me, looking direct into my eyes.

Tears welled up and chills rose through me. In that moment I knew. I was on track. And no matter how big the move was, I could do this.

[Quote from my book: *Open Me*]

Nature is speaking to us all the time.

Take 30 seconds to pause and be present with some part of nature: a tree, plant, clouds…and listen to what it has to say.

All of your emotions
are meant to flow
like a river.

#87
Let Your Emotions Flow

Our emotions are meant to flow just like a river.

When we suppress uncomfortable emotions, we block the natural flow of life force through the body and weaken it.

Like building a dam across the river–there are consequences to suppressing a natural flow.

When you lift the dam, the river flows. When you find a way to free the repressed emotions, you free up your body.

Your blood flows better. Your heart beats stronger. You feel more alive.

We are never truly feeling "nothing." When it seems that way, it often signals a stagnant pool of stuck emotion.

What gentle practices could help you to release repressed emotions? Journaling? Movement? Breathwork? Role play? Singing? Conversation?

#88
Waiting for Life to Happen

Lightning flashed, thunder roared, and the wind rose. I was so disappointed that my shamanic journey had been spoiled by the weather.

The rain pelted down. I wrapped the tarpaulin tighter around my head and neck preparing to wait out the storm for when I could continue my journey.

As I sat there shivering, I had another thought. How strange to think that I could press the pause button on life just because I didn't like what was going on.

I wondered how many other parts of my life I had on pause. Something inside me was beginning to wake up.

'What a waste of time to wait and not live until things get better!'

This was my shamanic journey, and I was missing it by waiting for something else to happen!

I decided that whatever was happening in each moment of my life, was an integral part of my journey.

[Quote from my book: *Real & Wild You*]

Have you been pressing pause somewhere in your life, because you don't want to deal with what's going on, instead of living it now?

We don't know how
this will go... but it
will be guided by
the frequency
in our heart.

#89
We Don't Know How This Will Go

Our world is changing: climate, biodiversity, authority structures, governance systems.

Our consciousness is shifting. People are more aware of what is going on in the world. More people are aware of realities that exist beyond the naked eye.

We don't really know how these changes will evolve. But one thing is certain. Energy goes where our attention is. And energy forms reality.

Keep your attention on your heart. It will guide this transformation.

We don't know how this will go…but it will be guided by the frequency in our heart.

What energy do you want to feed into the world today? Bring your attention there.

Believe you are enough...
right now... in this moment
and shatter the lies.

#90
You Are Enough

Believe you are enough…right now…in this moment and shatter the lies. You…are…divine and whole.

Simply your belief carries enough energy to override the old, habitual thoughts in your head.

Believe this. Again and again. And stand in the truth.

You are enough. You are whole. You are divine.

When my intuition is pointing to a particular path - and I take leaps to go on that path and trust - doors open.

#91
Take Leaps

*When my intuition is pointing to a particular path–
and I take leaps to go on that path and trust–doors
open.*

*As I keep taking leaps and trusting, particularly in the
face of no evidence that success is imminent, miracles
happen… and dreams are fulfilled.*

[Quote from my book: *Real & Wild You*]

Where could you trust more?

When I stop resisting
a situation, it can
often open up to
become an unexpected
gift.

#92
Be with What is Happening

When something happens that I don't like, I sometimes get upset.

But when I can *be with* what is happening around me... then I no longer resist it.

To *be with* something is to simply allow it to be there without any thought or attempt to change it.

In the absence of resistance, I have more attention and energy available–which frees up space in my mind to be resourceful instead of suffering.

When I stop resisting a situation, it can often open up to become an unexpected gift.

Is there something you are resisting that you could practice *being with* instead?

Embracing your shadow brings wholeness and peace.

#93
Face Your Shadow

I had come here to face the things I hated myself for—no matter how big or small anyone else thought they were.

I had come to face my shadow. I was not going to run away from her anymore.

I was going to stay right there and be with her, admit to her everything, and put my arms around her.

[Quote from my book: *Open Me*]

When we embrace those parts of ourselves we don't like, we end the inner struggle.

This brings peace. A natural feeling of wholeness arises.

We are always
being guided to
follow what is in
our highest good.

#94
Guided for Your Highest Good

I looked up. There was a cliff face to one side, like a mountain, and there were bushes below in the valley.

Tears filled my eyes. This was exactly what I had seen in my visions. I was overwhelmed with awe and gratitude that I had trusted my vision and listened to the forces guiding me through the unfamiliar canyon to this spot.

[Quote from my book: *Open Me*]

We are always being guided to follow what is for our highest good.

We only need to pay attention and listen.

Ask your Higher Self, "Where in my life right now, might I need to pause, listen, and trust more deeply?"

You don't want to get rid of the fear. You want to heal it and embrace it because you can.

#95
Your Fear is a Younger You

We often think we have to get rid of fear. But when we feel fear, unless it is a situation where your life is in danger, it is often a vulnerable and wounded part of yourself.

You don't want to get rid of the fear. You want to heal it and embrace it, because you can.

Consider your fear to be a much younger you who really needs a wise grown up to hold them and tell them they are safe. That's your job.

Trauma, which can be associated with the fear, triggers the cells of the body again and again until you interrupt them and help them to feel safe.

If my fear were a younger version of me, what would I want to say to help it feel safe?

Times of change are

the perfect opportunity
to break old habits and
create new ones.

#96
Times of Change Perfect
to Break Old Habits

Times of change are the perfect opportunity to break old habits and create new ones. Change naturally opens the door to new horizons.

But when a lot of change is happening, the ego-mind often resists—seeking control, clinging to the familiar, and slowing things down.

Yet breaking old patterns and forming new ones also reshapes the ego-mind itself. And because the ego resists change, things may feel uncomfortable, even overwhelming.

The ego may resist, but your true self is limitless. Change is the path that sets it free.

How open are you to the changes happening in your life?

#97
Slow Down and Listen

When you don't slow down to breathe, you can't easily hear, feel, or receive messages from your own deep wisdom.

Stop. Slow down. Listen.

What is your intuition whispering to you?

When you set an
intention for something
you want in your life,
the universe starts
conspiring for you.

#98
The Universe Conspires for You

When you set an intention for something you want in your life, the Universe starts conspiring for you.

This doesn't necessarily mean that circumstances organize themselves exactly how you want them to.

It is more likely that you will now attract the very circumstances that will help you to develop the skills and the ways of being required for you to live with this intention fulfilled.

You might also attract challenges to face, and as you deal with them, new opportunities may arise.

This is how it works.

But when we are in the thick of things, it can be helpful to remind ourselves of the intention we set that called in our circumstances.

You set an intention, consciously or unconsciously, that attracted what you are facing now. What might that intention be?

It isn't the (thing) you want. It's WHO YOU WILL BE as you reach for it.

#99
What You Really Want

It isn't the *thing* you want.

It isn't the degree, or the new body, or the new job, or a decluttered house … that you want.

It's the WHO YOU WILL BE as you reach for the BIG THING.

THAT is what you want.

If you imagine yourself now, already embodied in this version of yourself, who would you be in this now moment and how would that impact your next action?

Pay attention to the subtle. It is where the deepest richness of life exists.

#100
Pay Attention to the Subtle

Pay attention to the subtle.

Our culture praises speed, efficiency, and compliance—but in chasing these, we overlook what truly matters.

It is in the subtle—the quiet gestures, the soft textures, the rustle of leaves, the depth of color, the soft whispers of intuition, the pause between the notes, the still spaces—where the deepest richness of life exists.

Where in my life do I tend to rush past the subtle details?

Ask yourself, "Where could I pay more attention to the subtle and bring more richness into my life?"

About the Author

Leanne Babcock, Canadian-born, lived much of her life in New Zealand. She is a spiritual adventurer exploring the realms of consciousness and challenging the believed limits of reality.

A best-selling author, speaker and shamanic coach, she is also an NLP Master Practitioner trained in hypnotherapy, Master Coach in Multiple Brain Integration & a breathwork facilitator. Her work blends deep intuition, brain science and shamanic wisdom into a powerful fusion of transformation.

Following her heart's guidance, Leanne spends time in Canada and Mexico, remaining open to wherever spirit calls her next.

For over 30 years, she has led life-altering programs for people all around the world. She currently works with conscious women facilitating the space for generational trauma to release, for the mind to transform, for the heart to open, for consciousness to expand and for the soul to be set free.

To find out more about Leanne's work: leannebabcock.com

Other Books by Leanne Babcock

OPEN ME: The True Story of a Magical Journey from Fear to Freedom

A novel style real life story of betrayal, mystery, psychic phenomena, romance and adventure.

WILD & REAL YOU: Your Daring and Magical Inner Journey

An international best seller. A self-coaching guide into your mystical, inner depths.

www.ingramcontent.com/pod-product-compliance
Lightning Source LLC
Chambersburg PA
CBHW060418130626
46555CB00005B/2111